Red Kangaroo

Greg Pyers

ECHIDNA BOOKS

First published 2004 by Echidna Books
an imprint of Harcourt Education
18–22 Salmon Street, Port Melbourne, Victoria, 3207, Australia
(a division of Reed International Books Australia Pty Ltd, ABN 70 001 002 357)
A Reed Elsevier company
Website   www.heinemannlibrary.com.au

Produced by Binara Publishing Pty Ltd
247 Cardigan Street, Carlton, Victoria, 3053
ABN 76 657 508 297

08 07 06 05 04
10 9 8 7 6 5 4 3 2 1

Series design by David Doyle
Edited by Jaclyn Crupi
Picture research by Jaclyn Crupi
Illustrations by Andrew Plant
Film separations by Show-Ads, Melbourne
Printed in China by Wing King Tong

National Library of Australia Cataloguing-in-publication data:

Pyers, Greg.
Red kangaroo.

For primary school students.

ISBN 1 74070 801 6.

1. Kangaroos – Australia – Juvenile literature.
I. Title. (Series : Life cycles of Australian animals).

599.22230994

Pictures: Lochman Transparencies: pages 15 (Wade Hughes), 23 (Dennis Sarson), 29 (Jiri Lochman).
Nature Focus – Australian Museum: page 25 (Dave Watts). ANT Photo Library. pages 5, 9, 27 (Otto
Rogge). 7 and front cover (Dave Watts), 11 (Jack Cameron), 13 (NHPA), 17 (Dick Whitford),
19 (Peter McDonald), 21 (Martin Harvey).

132/Files pg5 rk01; pg7 rk02; pg9 rk03; pg11 rk04; pg13 rk05; pg15 rk06; pg17 rk07; pg19 rk08;
pg 21 rk09; pg23 rk10; pg25 rk11; pg27 rk12; pg29 rk13

Contents

The biggest marsupial

A kind of mammal

A red kangaroo is a **mammal**. Mammals are animals whose first food is milk from their mothers. But a red kangaroo is a special kind of mammal. It is a **marsupial**.

Marsupials

Marsupials are mammals whose young develop in a pouch. Other mammal babies are quite well developed when they are born. Some, such as horses, can run within minutes of birth. Marsupial babies, however, are born at a very early stage of development. Most of a marsupial baby's development occurs after birth, in its mother's pouch.

All sorts of pouches

Different kinds of marsupials have different kinds of pouches. The kultarr, a small desert mouse, develops a pouch only in the breeding season. Wombat pouches open to the rear.

When the female red kangaroo is ready to give birth she cleans her pouch.

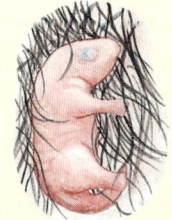
The tiny **joey** is born about 33 days after its parents **mate**. It climbs to the pouch.

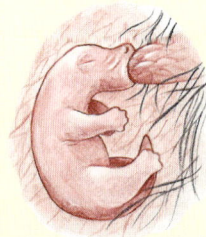
The newborn joey attaches to a teat in its mother's pouch and drinks milk.

A male red kangaroo. The red kangaroo
is the largest marsupial of all.

The joey first sticks its head
out of the pouch when it is
about five months old.

At about eight months of age the
joey is too big for the pouch, but it
will drink milk until it is a year old.

Red kangaroos reach
adulthood at about two
years old.

Living together

Groups and mobs

Red kangaroos are usually found in groups of two or three. These groups may belong to a mob of 20 or more that has spread out to feed over a wide area.

Size and colour

Telling males and females apart is easy. Adult males are about twice the size of adult females, and only females have pouches.

Males are usually red, and females are usually a blueish colour, which is why they are sometimes called 'blue-fliers'.

Advantages of group living

Living in groups has advantages. Males and females are close together so they can breed at any time of the year. Being part of a group also means that there are many eyes and ears alert for **predators**.

When the female red kangaroo is ready to give birth she cleans her pouch.

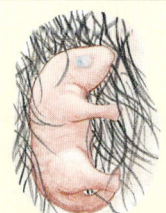

The tiny **joey** is born about 33 days after its parents **mate**. It climbs to the pouch.

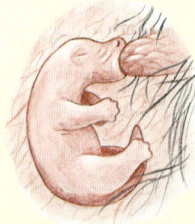

The newborn joey attaches to a teat in its mother's pouch and drinks milk.

A female (lying down), her **joey** (now too big
for her pouch) and a male red kangaroo

The joey first sticks its head
out of the pouch when it is
about five months old.

At about eight months of age the
joey is too big for the pouch, but it
will drink milk until it is a year old.

Red kangaroos reach
adulthood at about two
years old.

Where red kangaroos live

Arid zone

Red kangaroos live right across Australia's vast **arid zone**. The land is wide and flat, rainfall is low and plants are sparse. **Droughts** are frequent.

Adaptations

To survive, the red kangaroo has many features that suit it very well to living in such a habitat. These features are called adaptations. One adaptation is the red kangaroo's habit of licking its forearms in very hot weather. This helps it to cool down. Red kangaroos also dig into the hot soil so that they can lie in the cooler soil below the surface.

Feeding and resting

Red kangaroos feed from late afternoon, through the night and into early morning. During the hottest part of the day they rest in shade. They also rest on cold winter nights.

When the female red kangaroo is ready to give birth she cleans her pouch.

The tiny **joey** is born about 33 days after its parents **mate**. It climbs to the pouch.

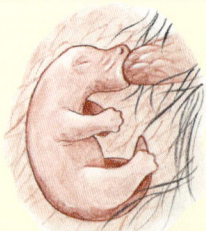

The newborn joey attaches to a teat in its mother's pouch and drinks milk.

Red kangaroos live in Australia's arid zone where rainfall is low and unreliable.

The joey first sticks its head out of the pouch when it is about five months old.

At about eight months of age the joey is too big for the pouch, but it will drink milk until it is a year old.

Red kangaroos reach adulthood at about two years old.

Close to home

Red kangaroos spend most of their time **foraging** within an area often no larger than five square kilometres.

They eat green leaves and shoots, which are often in short supply during dry spells. Amazingly, if rain falls elsewhere, red kangaroos seem to know and will travel 50 kilometres or more to feed on the new growth.

Water shortages

Red kangaroos can get by on one drink a week. But in times of **drought**, they stop producing young.

Plenty of water

Sheep and cattle farmers in inland Australia have dug bores to provide water for their stock. These new water sources allow red kangaroos to produce **joeys** in dry years. Because of this, there are now more red kangaroos than ever.

When the female red kangaroo is ready to give birth she cleans her pouch.

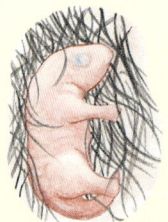

The tiny **joey** is born about 33 days after its parents **mate**. It climbs to the pouch.

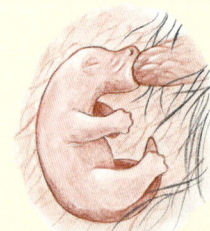

The newborn joey attaches to a teat in its mother's pouch and drinks milk.

A mob drinking at a waterhole. In times of drought, red kangaroos stay close to water sources that haven't dried up.

The joey first sticks its head out of the pouch when it is about five months old.

At about eight months of age the joey is too big for the pouch, but it will drink milk until it is a year old.

Red kangaroos reach adulthood at about two years old.

Producing young

Reproduction

Reproduction means producing and raising young. A female red kangaroo usually **mates** with the **dominant** male of the mob.

After mating, a male red kangaroo plays no part in the raising of the young – this is done by the mother.

Choosing the right time

Red kangaroos can produce young at any time of the year.

This allows red kangaroos to have young when food is plentiful, and not to have young when food is scarce. In good years, a female red kangaroo may have a **joey** developing in her pouch, an older joey out of her pouch, and be pregnant as well.

Gestation

Gestation is the length of time a female is pregnant. In red kangaroos, this is normally 33 days.

When the female red kangaroo is ready to give birth she cleans her pouch.

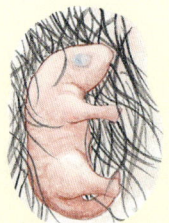

The tiny **joey** is born about 33 days after its parents **mate**. It climbs to the pouch.

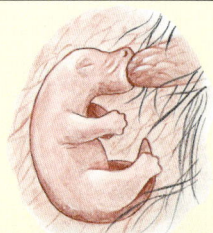

The newborn joey attaches to a teat in its mother's pouch and drinks milk.

When male red kangaroos fight it is to decide who is dominant – usually the largest and strongest.

The joey first sticks its head out of the pouch when it is about five months old.

At about eight months of age the joey is too big for the pouch, but it will drink milk until it is a year old.

Red kangaroos reach adulthood at about two years old.

A joey is born

A tiny animal

A newborn red kangaroo is a very tiny animal. Its first few minutes of life are risky. Its mother has to give it the best chance of surviving this difficult time.

Preparations

When a pregnant female is about to give birth, she finds a secluded place where she can be on her own. She sits upright with her tail between her hind legs and her back leaning against a tree or shrub. Now she licks her pouch. She has been cleaning her pouch in this way for a few days now. Just before the birth, she licks her **cloaca**, the opening through which the baby will be born.

Birth

The tiny baby is born in just a few seconds. It is in a clear fluid-filled sac, which breaks as it is born.

When the female red kangaroo is ready to give birth she cleans her pouch.

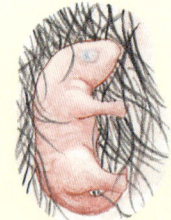

The tiny **joey** is born about 33 days after its parents **mate**. It climbs to the pouch.

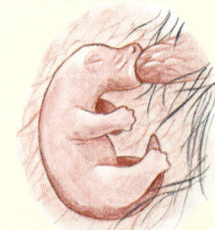

The newborn joey attaches to a teat in its mother's pouch and drinks milk.

This female is cleaning her pouch. When she is ready to give birth, she will move away to be by herself.

The joey first sticks its head out of the pouch when it is about five months old.

At about eight months of age the joey is too big for the pouch, but it will drink milk until it is a year old.

Red kangaroos reach adulthood at about two years old.

Just born

A still baby

For a few moments after it is born, the newborn kangaroo is still. It doesn't look much like a red kangaroo at all, with its pink, hairless body and stumps for hind legs. But its front legs are quite well developed, and it soon starts to use them.

A long climb

The newborn breaks free of the sac and grasps at its mother's fur with its strong front paws. Instinctively, it climbs upwards, away from the pull of gravity, while the mother licks up the birth fluids. The baby reaches up with one arm and then the other, hauling itself through the fur. After three minutes, it reaches the pouch and disappears inside.

Breaking the cord

The umbilical cord, which attached the unborn **embryo** to its mother's **placenta**, breaks as the newborn climbs.

When the female red kangaroo is ready to give birth she cleans her pouch.

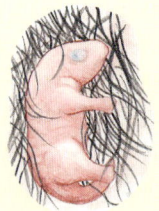

The tiny **joey** is born about 33 days after its parents **mate**. It climbs to the pouch.

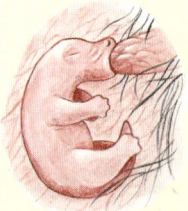

The newborn joey attaches to a teat in its mother's pouch and drinks milk.

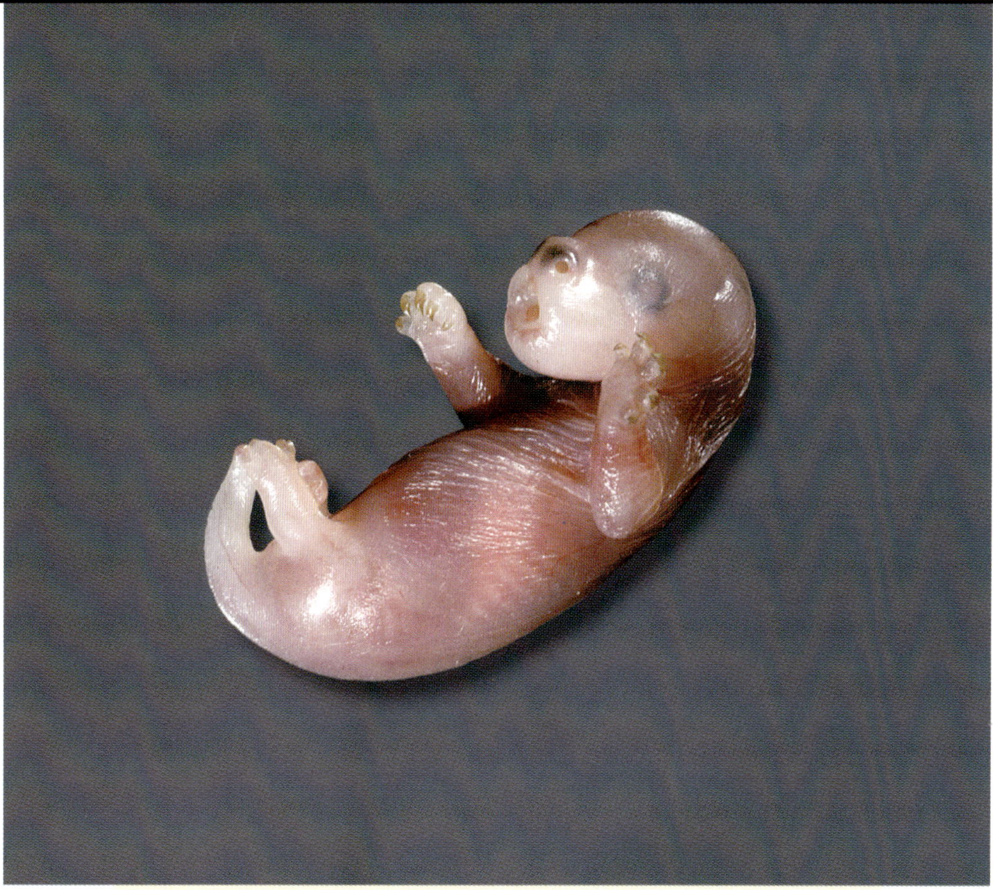

A newborn red kangaroo is just two centimetres
long – the size of a jellybean.

The joey first sticks its head
out of the pouch when it is
about five months old.

At about eight months of age the
joey is too big for the pouch, but it
will drink milk until it is a year old.

Red kangaroos reach
adulthood at about two
years old.

Milk

Finding a nipple

At the entrance to the pouch, the newborn uses its sense of smell to find its way down to one of its mother's four nipples. Within a few minutes, the newborn has attached its mouth to one of the nipples and begins to **suckle**.

Changing milk

The first milk drunk by the newborn has many **antibodies** in it. These protect the growing **joey** from infection.

As the joey grows, the quantity of milk increases. The amount of fat in the milk also increases, to provide more energy.

Milk for everyone

With a tiny joey in her pouch, the female may also have an older joey that has left the pouch. Each joey requires a different type and amount of milk. Amazingly, the mother can provide both.

When the female red kangaroo is ready to give birth she cleans her pouch.

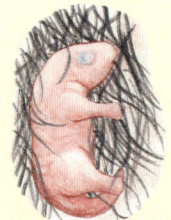

The tiny joey is born about 33 days after its parents **mate**. It climbs to the pouch.

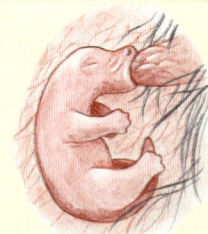

The newborn joey attaches to a teat in its mother's pouch and drinks milk.

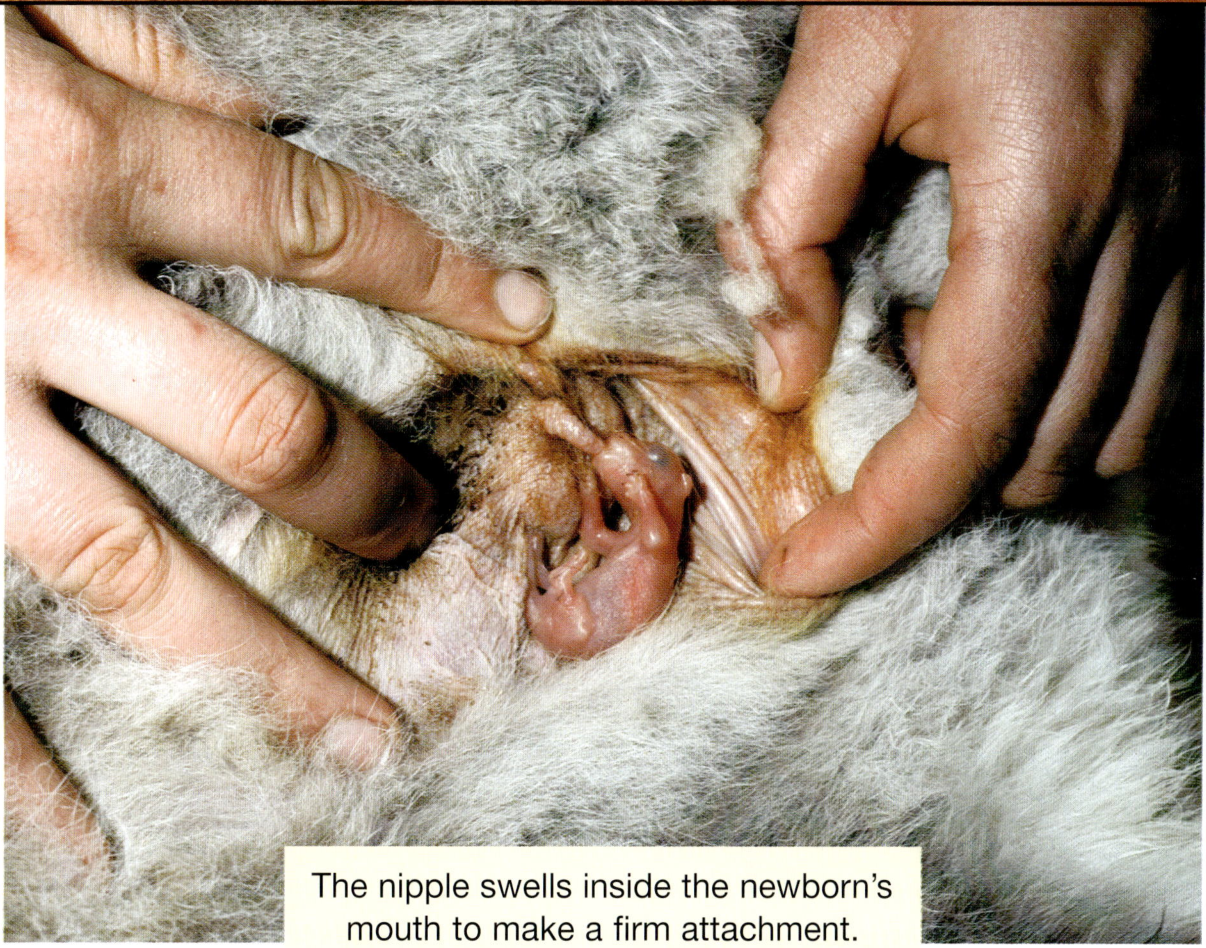

The nipple swells inside the newborn's mouth to make a firm attachment. This joey is about three weeks old.

The joey first sticks its head out of the pouch when it is about five months old.

At about eight months of age the joey is too big for the pouch, but it will drink milk until it is a year old.

Red kangaroos reach adulthood at about two years old.

Life in a pouch

Development

The young, hairless **joey** grows slowly in the first few weeks. But about 14 weeks after birth, the joey has a growth spurt. It is still almost completely hairless, but its tail, claws, ears and hind legs are well developed. Its eyes will soon be open.

First appearance

When the joey is about 21 weeks old, its eyes have opened. It now pokes its head out for its first look at the world. But the joey has only a very light covering of hair and so it needs to stay in the warmth of the pouch for a little while yet.

Cleaning up

By licking her joey's rear end, the mother stimulates the joey to pass urine and faeces. She consumes the baby's wastes and keeps her pouch clean.

When the female red kangaroo is ready to give birth she cleans her pouch.

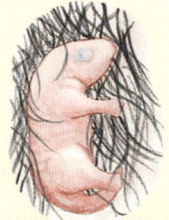

The tiny joey is born about 33 days after its parents **mate**. It climbs to the pouch.

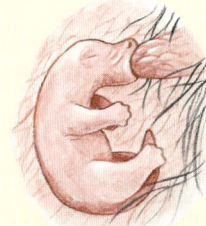

The newborn joey attaches to a teat in its mother's pouch and drinks milk.

The pouch provides warmth and protection for a red kangaroo joey until it is eight months old.

The joey first sticks its head out of the pouch when it is about five months old.

At about eight months of age the joey is too big for the pouch, but it will drink milk until it is a year old.

Red kangaroos reach adulthood at about two years old.

In and out of the pouch

The first time out

The **joey** ventures out of the pouch for the first time when it is about 27 weeks old. But it stays out only for about one minute. Over the next few weeks, it will make many more excursions out of the pouch, slowly getting used to jumping around on its huge hind legs.

Getting back in

If danger threatens, the joey's mother calls with a kind of cough. She relaxes muscles at the lip of the pouch and leans forward to let her youngster dive in headfirst. She then tightens the pouch muscles to keep the joey in.

Time in the pouch

Different kinds of kangaroos spend different amounts of time in the pouch. A western grey kangaroo joey doesn't leave its mother's pouch until it is at least 37 weeks old.

When the female red kangaroo is ready to give birth she cleans her pouch.

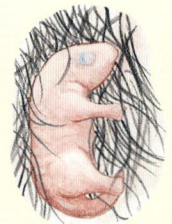

The tiny joey is born about 33 days after its parents **mate**. It climbs to the pouch.

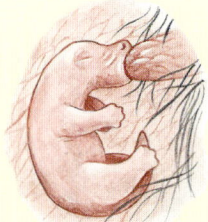

The newborn joey attaches to a teat in its mother's pouch and drinks milk.

A red kangaroo joey taking a drink from its mother.
This joey is almost old enough to stop drinking milk.

The joey first sticks its head out of the pouch when it is about five months old.

At about eight months of age the joey is too big for the pouch, but it will drink milk until it is a year old.

Red kangaroos reach adulthood at about two years old.

Leaving the pouch for good

Too big for the pouch

When a **joey** is about 34 weeks old and weighs 4.5 kilograms, it is too large for its mother to carry. When it tries to get inside her pouch, she may move away or tighten her pouch muscles to keep the entrance closed. After a few days, the joey stops trying to get in.

Weaning

The joey is eating quite a bit of grass now, but it continues to drink milk for another four months. Towards the end of this time, the joey **suckles** less frequently. Then, when it is about one year old, its mother stops feeding it altogether. The joey is now **weaned**.

A new joey

If conditions are right, a female red kangaroo can give birth to a new joey within four days of a joey leaving the pouch for good.

When the female red kangaroo is ready to give birth she cleans her pouch.

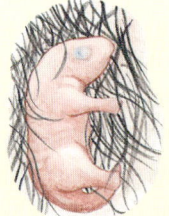

The tiny joey is born about 33 days after its parents **mate**. It climbs to the pouch.

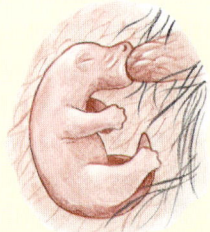

The newborn joey attaches to a teat in its mother's pouch and drinks milk.

A mother gently pushes her joey away to keep it from trying to drink from her.

The joey first sticks its head out of the pouch when it is about five months old.

At about eight months of age the joey is too big for the pouch, but it will drink milk until it is a year old.

Red kangaroos reach adulthood at about two years old.

Fully grown

Leaving mum

Until a red kangaroo is old enough to have young of its own, it might continue to stay close to its mother. The age at which a red kangaroo is mature and ready to **mate** varies. If conditions are right, a red kangaroo can breed by the time it is two years old.

Growing

Red kangaroos continue to grow for most of their lives. A male, for example, weighs about 25 kilograms at three years, 40 kilograms at five and 70 kilograms at 10 years.

Jumping

Jumping is an energy efficient way of travelling long distances at high speeds. However, it is not energy-efficient for moving slowly. At these times, the kangaroo moves by putting its weight on its front paws and tail, and then swinging its hind legs forward.

When the female red kangaroo is ready to give birth she cleans her pouch.

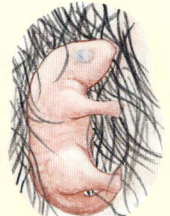

The tiny **joey** is born about 33 days after its parents mate. It climbs to the pouch.

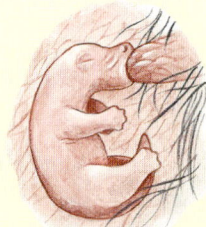

The newborn joey attaches to a teat in its mother's pouch and drinks milk.

The red kangaroo's heavy tail is essential for keeping balance when bounding at high speed.

The joey first sticks its head out of the pouch when it is about five months old.

At about eight months of age the joey is too big for the pouch, but it will drink milk until it is a year old.

Red kangaroos reach adulthood at about two years old.

Predators and other dangers

Dingoes

Dingoes hunt red kangaroos. They work in packs to run down their prey. Usually, it is the slowest kangaroos that are caught by dingoes. These are the ones that are old or injured or carrying **joeys**.

Humans

Aboriginal people of central Australia have hunted red kangaroos for many centuries. They used the meat for food, the hides for clothing and even the **tendons** for string. Kangaroo meat is also sold in butcher shops and restaurants, and as food for pets.

Hunting numbers

Each year, the Federal Government decides how many red kangaroos can be killed by hunters. This number is called a **quota**. The quota changes each year, depending on the estimated number of red kangaroos in the wild.

When the female red kangaroo is ready to give birth she cleans her pouch.

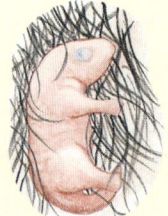

The tiny **joey** is born about 33 days after its parents **mate**. It climbs to the pouch.

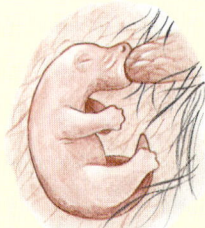

The newborn joey attaches to a teat in its mother's pouch and drinks milk.

Wedge-tailed eagles may sometimes catch a joey.
This eagle is eating a red kangaroo killed on the road.

The joey first sticks its head
out of the pouch when it is
about five months old.

At about eight months of age the
joey is too big for the pouch, but it
will drink milk until it is a year old.

Red kangaroos reach
adulthood at about two
years old.

Red kangaroo facts

Red kangaroo names

The word 'kangaroo' was first recorded by Captain James Cook, after hearing the name from Aboriginal people in northern Queensland. Aboriginal people in central Australia called this animal 'marloo'.

Scientific name: *Macropus rufus*. *Macropus* means 'large foot'; *rufus* means 'red'.

Northern Territory

Queensland

Western Australia

South Australia

New South Wales

N

0   500km

Victoria

ACT

Tasmania

● Where red kangaroos can be found

Size

Weight:

males – up to 85 kg

females – up to 35 kg

joey just out of the pouch – 2 kg

Head and body length:

males – up to 1.4 m

females – up to 1 m

Tail length:

males – up to 1 m

females – up to 90 cm

Endangered?

Red kangaroos are not endangered. It is estimated that there are about eight million red kangaroos in Australia today.

Marsupials

'Marsupial' comes from a Latin word *marsupium*, meaning 'pouch'.

More than half of the world's 230 species of marsupials live in Australia.

Glossary

antibodies   cells that help prevent or overcome infection

arid zone   the dry, desert area of Australia

cloaca   the opening through which the female red kangaroo gives birth

dominant   usually the largest and strongest animal in a group

drought   an extended period of below-average rainfall

embryo   an undeveloped young inside its mother or inside an egg

foraging   hunting or searching for food

gestation   the length of time of pregnancy

joey   a young kangaroo

mammal   an animal whose first food is milk from its mother

marsupial   a mammal that is born at a very undeveloped stage and which continues its development inside its mother's pouch

mate   the joining of a male and female so that sperm can be passed from the male to the female

placenta   the organ inside a pregnant mammal that supplies the embryo with nutrients

predator   an animal that kills and eats other animals

quota   the yearly level set by the Government for the number of red kangaroos that may be killed by licensed kangaroo shooters

suckle   to drink milk from a mother's nipple

tendons   strong fibres that attach muscles to bones

weaned   when a mammal stops drinking milk from its mother

Find out more

Pearson, J. *Australian Animals – Mammals*, Heinemann Library, Melbourne, 1999.

Pyers, G. *How Animals and Plants Survive in Australia's Deserts*, Heinemann Library, Melbourne, 2003.

Index